ANNE AND HER TOWER OF GIRAFFES

The Adventurous Life of the First Giraffologist

For my parents, Dan and Vicki Gray.
And with gratitude to the unstoppable
Dr. Anne Innis Dagg. — K.G.
To my fond memories of Africa — A.V.

What Is the Plural of *Giraffe*?

Both *giraffe* and *giraffes* are correct when referring to more than one.
Dr. Dagg uses *giraffe* both in speaking and in print. But for consistency
throughout this book (and with Dr. Dagg's permission), the author
added an *s* to Dr. Dagg's quotes about giraffes. And what's
another word for a group of giraffes? A TOWER!

Text © 2022 Karlin Gray
Illustrations © 2022 Aparna Varma

Published in Canada and the U.S. by Kids Can Press Ltd.
25 Dockside Drive, Toronto, ON M5A 0B5

Kids Can Press is a Corus Entertainment Inc. company

www.kidscanpress.com

The artwork in this book was rendered in colored pencils and Photoshop.
The text is set in Absent Grotesque.

Edited by Jennifer Stokes and Katie Scott
Designed by Michael Reis

Printed and bound in Buji, Shenzhen, China, in 3/2022 by WKT Company

CM 22 0 9 8 7 6 5 4 3 2 1

Library and Archives Canada Cataloguing in Publication

Title: Anne and her tower of giraffes : the adventurous life of the first giraffologist /
written by Karlin Gray ; illustrated by Aparna Varma.
Names: Gray, Karlin, author. | Varma, Aparna, illustrator.
Description: Includes bibliographical references.
Identifiers: Canadiana 20210360119 | ISBN 9781525304958 (hardcover)
Subjects: LCSH: Dagg, Anne Innis — Juvenile literature. | LCSH: Women zoologists — Canada —
Biography — Juvenile literature. | LCSH: Zoologists — Canada — Biography — Juvenile literature. |
LCSH: Giraffe — Africa — Juvenile literature. | LCGFT: Biographies
Classification: LCC QL31.D34 G73 2022 | DDC j590.92 — dc23

Kids Can Press gratefully acknowledges that the land on which our office is located
is the traditional territory of many nations, including the Mississaugas of the Credit,
the Anishnabeg, the Chippewa, the Haudenosaunee and the Wendat peoples, and is
now home to many diverse First Nations, Inuit and Métis peoples.

We thank the Government of Ontario, through Ontario Creates; the Ontario
Arts Council; the Canada Council for the Arts; and the Government of Canada
for supporting our publishing activity.

ANNE AND HER TOWER OF GIRAFFES

The Adventurous Life of the First Giraffologist

Written by Karlin Gray

Illustrated by Aparna Varma

KIDS CAN PRESS

Four-year-old Anne explored the many wonders at Chicago's Brookfield Zoo until ...

her bright blue eyes spotted a towering, elegant creature.

Wow!

Anne gazed into the giraffe's big brown eyes and refused to leave. Eventually, her mother insisted — time to go!

But the memory of the beautiful giraffe
followed her home to Toronto.

Anne drew picture after picture of her giraffe.
She wanted to know EVERYTHING about it.

What do giraffes eat?
Do they make noises?
Why are their necks so long?

Growing up, she found plenty of
library books about beavers, deer
and even elephants, but NOTHING
about giraffes.

ANIMALS

READING TAKES
YOU AROUND
THE WORLD!

Anne made a promise: one day, *she*
would write a book all about giraffes.
Her friends were amused.

Anne loved going to school, always hoping her studies would include the long-necked creature with the big brown eyes.

Maybe this year,
I'll learn something
about giraffes.

But each year, Anne was
disappointed.

Just before she turned twelve, Anne caught scarlet fever. Stuck in a hospital bed, she celebrated her birthday alone until ... three tiny visitors appeared!

Finally, after a month in the hospital, Anne felt better and packed her bag. But the nurse had bad news: because they didn't want germs to spread and infect others, they had to destroy all of Anne's belongings — including her giraffes!

Anne pleaded desperately on behalf of her new friends.

Scrubbed clean, three little giraffes followed Anne home.

At seventeen, Anne returned to the zoo. This time, a giraffe walked straight toward Anne and dipped his head over the fence.

Bright blues peered into big browns.

Anne's love of giraffes guided her to a university to study zoology. Surely, she'd learn about her favorite animal there!

But again, Anne was disappointed.

Anne couldn't wait any longer. She made a decision: if she couldn't find a way to study giraffes at home, she would travel to the giraffes' true home — the continent of Africa.

And that made *a lot* of people laugh.

A woman traveling across the world on her own? A woman studying animals in the wild? Unheard of!

But their laughter just made Anne more determined. She wrote letter after letter requesting help from national parks and game reserves.

One day, she received a life-changing reply from a ranch in South Africa where more than one hundred giraffes roamed free. She couldn't wait to tell her mother.

I can stay at this place — Fleur de Lys Ranch — while I watch giraffes EVERY day!

In the summer of 1956, Anne set off for a year of study, traveling by passenger ship from Canada to England ... from England to South Africa.

With another thousand miles left to travel, Anne bought a used car and named it Camelo — short for the giraffe's scientific name, *Giraffa camelopardalis*.

At last, I'm in Africa!

After days of driving in the intense
heat, she arrived at the ranch and was
greeted by the owner, Mr. Matthew.

Welcome to
Fleur de Lys Ranch!

In the morning, Mr. Matthew offered Anne his binoculars, a film recorder and a drive to see her first giraffe in the wild.

The moment I've been waiting for my whole life!

They stopped near a pool of water
where several animals gathered.
One, two, three, four antelopes and ...

a huge
giraffe!

Bright blues peered
into big browns.

She's gorgeous!

Every day, from dawn to dusk, Anne
and Camelo went giraffing.

Anne sought out the best places to
observe giraffes and learned how to
identify each one. Memorizing their
markings, she named them all …

Pom Pom: prominent horn hairs
The Twins: close buddies
Cream: a cream rather than a white background
Lumpy: lumps on his lower neck
Limpy: a snare embedded in his lower leg
Pim: gentle
Blond: a light-colored bull
Star: body spots with jagged edges

Anne recorded all of her observations on giraffe behavior — from their diets ... to their vocal noises ... to their movements.

Giraffes eat acacia leaves.

Ha, ha. I've read that giraffes never make any vocal noises but now I know that's wrong.

SNORT

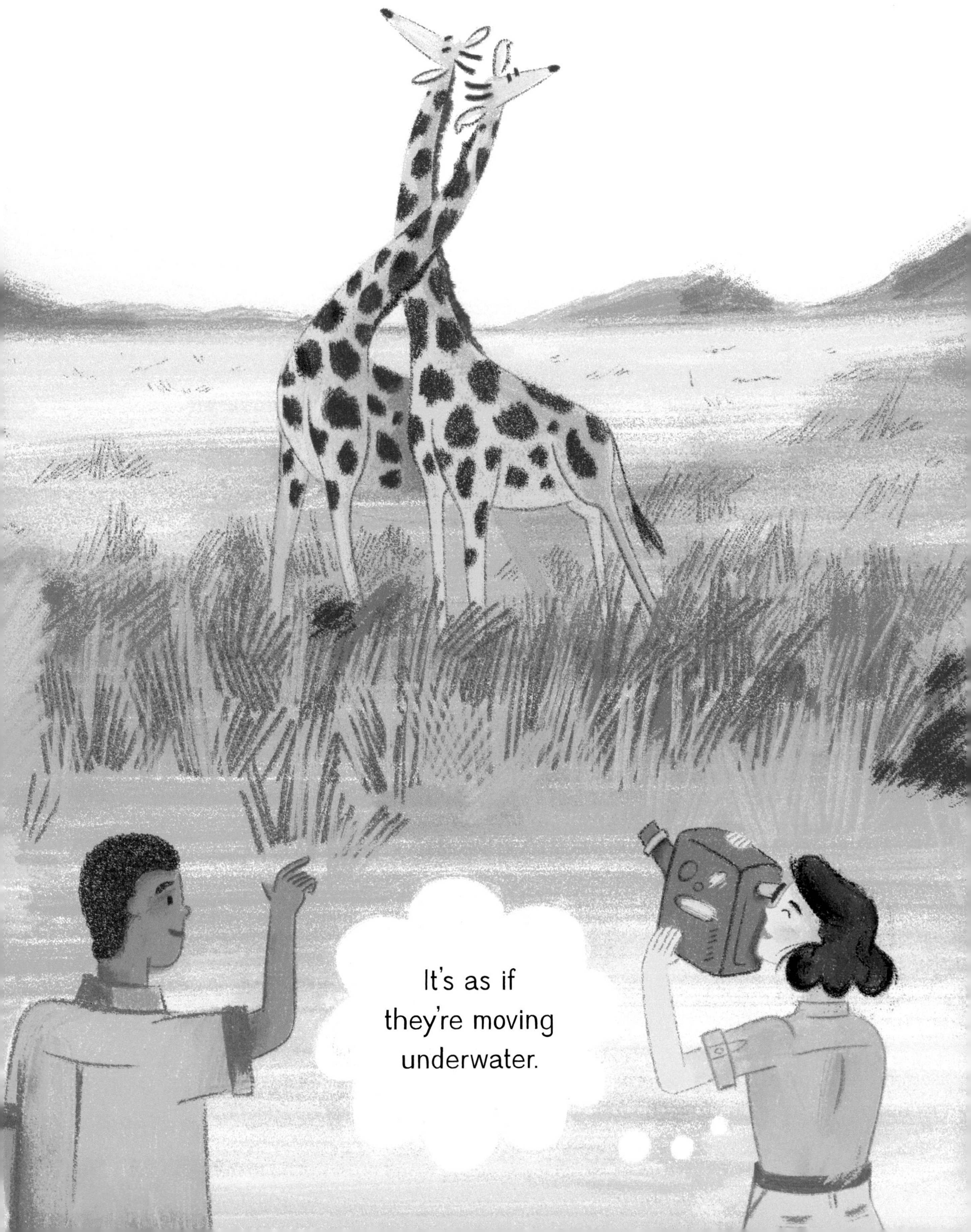
It's as if they're moving underwater.

Sometimes, she thought
she was observing one
giraffe, but really a group
of giraffes — a "tower" —
watched over Anne.

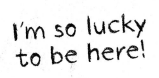

Eventually, Anne's year of study was over — time to go.

Trying not to cry, Anne left South Africa. But the memory of Pom Pom, The Twins, Cream, Lumpy, Limpy, Pim, Blond and Star followed her home.

Back home, Anne couldn't wait to tell the world what she had learned. But when she applied for jobs as a full-time professor, the universities just laughed at her. And that laughter *stung*.

Even though Anne was the first Western scientist to study giraffes in the wild, no one would hire her as a professor because those jobs were given to men.

Anne challenged their decision for years but lost. And then she remembered her childhood promise. If she couldn't share her knowledge as a professor, she'd do it as ...

a writer!

Over time, Anne went on to write more than twenty books! She wrote about giraffes, animal behavior, women's rights, the environment — and even a book for children, just like the one she had searched for all those years ago.

Eventually, Anne's adventures caught the attention of someone who turned Anne's story into ...

a movie! Now even more people could learn about giraffes. And that made Anne laugh with joy.

NOW PLAYING

THE WOMAN WHO LOVES GIRAFFES

THE STORY OF ANNE INNIS DAGG

Author's Note

> **"** All I ever wanted to be when I was growing up was a person who studied giraffes. **"**
>
> — Dr. Anne Innis Dagg

Born in 1933 to an American writer and a Canadian economics professor, Anne Innis grew up the youngest of four children in Toronto, Canada. She went on to receive degrees in biology, genetics and animal behavior. Her solo trip to South Africa in 1956 made her the first Western person to study wild animal behavior in Africa. A few years later, trailblazers in primate studies followed: Jane Goodall studied chimpanzees, Dian Fossey researched mountain gorillas and Biruté Galdikas learned all about orangutans.

Back in Canada, Anne married physicist Ian Dagg, had three children and looked forward to a life of teaching. However, even though she was a pioneer in giraffe study, Anne faced gender discrimination when she applied for jobs as a professor and never received tenure (a permanent position as a university professor). Anne was heartbroken but persistent. She published her research extensively and wrote the first scientific book on giraffes, which inspired future generations to study and protect the world's tallest land animal.

Following the release of Alison Reid's 2018 documentary on Dr. Dagg, *The Woman Who Loves Giraffes*, one university issued an apology for denying Anne tenure and created a research

> **"** I am thrilled to have the baby named after me and so excited. Every night when I go to sleep, I will wonder what my new little girl will be doing. **"**
>
> — Dr. Anne Innis Dagg

scholarship in her honor. And in 2020, a baby giraffe at the Toronto Zoo was named Amani Innis Dagg.

Over the years, the giraffe population has declined drastically, and they are now listed as "vulnerable to extinction" — one ranking below "endangered." In response, Anne created a foundation to work with the local community and educate young people on how to help giraffes survive and thrive in the wild. To learn more about Dr. Dagg and giraffe conservation, visit www.anneinnisdaggfoundation.org.

" If we don't do enough to save them, then giraffes will be gone forever. What an awful thought, that there might never be any giraffes in the whole world! **"**

— Dr. Anne Innis Dagg

A Note about Apartheid

Anne's 1956 trip to South Africa took place during apartheid — the country's policy of segregating people by race. While Anne was grateful for her time at the Fleur de Lys Ranch, she detested the country's racist policies and was criticized for socializing and working with Black people. In her memoir *Pursuing Giraffe: A 1950s Adventure*, Anne documents her observations of the country's racial relations at that time and shares her views of an unjust system.

" How could it be that some people were denied schooling because of the color of their skin? And then were derided because of their lack of education? **"**

— Dr. Anne Innis Dagg

An Interview with Dr. Anne Innis Dagg

Q: When people laughed at your dream to study the giraffe, how did you react?

A: I just ignored them as silly people. I knew what I was going to do.

Q: Do you still have the giraffes your mother made you when you were in the hospital with scarlet fever?

A: I still have one who is looking rather bedraggled from being loved by my own three kids over the years.

Q: What has a lifetime of studying giraffes given you personally?

A: Much joy and, recently, many, many friends who also love giraffes.

Q: If you could tell your childhood self anything, what would it be?

A: If you want to be a biologist, keep notes on everything you can think of. Often, you will wish you had if you do not.

Q: After the premiere of the documentary *The Woman Who Loves Giraffes*, what went through your mind as you stood on stage and looked out at the audience cheering you on?

A: After the movie premiere, when the whole audience of about one hundred people stood up and clapped like mad, I was thrilled that the giraffes in Africa have more hope of surviving than I had imagined. It was perhaps the best moment of my life, that I had been involved in making the film and it had come off so well!

Q: What is it like to meet kids today who share your love of the giraffe?

A: I love to meet young people who are interested in animals. It means so much for the future and will bring such happiness to the children as they grow up.

Resources for Kids

Dagg, Anne Innis. *5 Giraffes*. Toronto: Fitzhenry & Whiteside, 2016.

Junior Giraffe Club (Anne Innis Dagg Foundation): www.juniorgiraffeclub.org

Stinson, Kathy. *The Girl Who Loved Giraffes: And Became the World's First Giraffologist*. Toronto: Fitzhenry & Whiteside, 2021.

Author's Sources

In researching this book, the author interviewed Dr. Anne Innis Dagg by email. Direct quotes from this interview are found on pages 27 and 41.

Books

Dagg, Anne Innis. *Pursuing Giraffe: A 1950s Adventure*. (Kindle Edition) Waterloo: Wilfred Laurier University Press, 2006. Direct quotes from this source on pages 20, 21, 25, 27, 28, 29 and 41.

Dagg, Anne Innis. *Smitten by Giraffe: My Life as a Citizen Scientist*. Montreal: McGill-Queen's University Press, 2016. Direct quotes from this source on pages 19 and 31.

Film

Reid, Alison, dir. *The Woman Who Loves Giraffes: The Story of Anne Innis Dagg*. Pursuing Giraffe Adventures Inc. and Free Spirit Films, 2018. Direct quote from this source on page 22.

News Reports

Alozzi, Raneem. "This Little Giraffe Has a Big Name: Toronto Zoo's 'Baby Long Legs' Now Goes by Amani Innis Dagg." *The Toronto Star*, June 21, 2020. Direct quote from this source on page 40.

Dagg, Anne Innis. "I Made It Through Scarlet Fever, and So Did My Stuffed Giraffes." *The Toronto Star*, May 2, 2020.

"Wild Journey: The Anne Innis Story." CBC Radio, *Ideas*, January 30, 2014 (audio). Direct quotes from this source on pages 5 and 11.

Tremonti, Anna Maria. *The Current*, CBC Radio, February 18, 2019, episode (transcript).

Websites

Anne Innis Dagg Foundation (official website of Dr. Anne Innis Dagg): www.anneinnisdaggfoundation.org. Direct quote from this source on page 40.

The Woman Who Loves Giraffes (official website of the documentary): www.thewomanwholovesgiraffes.com